Pillowslips

Gasmasks

Liverpool's Wartime Evacuation

by

Joan Boyce

Illustrations Acknowledgements

Sincere thanks to the following for permission to reproduce illustrations:

Liverpool City Libraries — Frontispiece and 2, 3, 9, 10, 11, 12, 13.

Liverpool City Engineers Dept. — 6.

The Hulton-Deutsch Collection Ltd. — 14, 21.

Mrs. E. Bywater — 4, 5.

Mr. and Mrs. Dillon — 15.

Joan Boyce — 18, 19, 20.

Arnold Derrington — 17.

First published 1989 by Liver Press, 1 & 3 Grove Road, Rock Ferry, Birkenhead, Wirral, Merseyside L42 3XS.

Copyright © Joan Boyce, 1989.
Typeset in the University of Liverpool and printed by Birkenhead Press Limited, 1 & 3 Grove Road, Rock Ferry, Birkenhead, Merseyside L42 3XS.

ISBN 1 871201 02 0.

Contents

To my grandsons Joe (aged 4)
and Aidan (aged 18 months)

God shall quell the world's quarrels -
even among distant empires:
sword and spear shall be forged
into ploughshare and pruning knife:
there shall be no more war,
no more training camps,
no more parade grounds!
(from the Old Testament)

Acknowledgements

I would like to express my sincere thanks to all who have assisted in the writing of this book. First place should be given to the former evacuees who gave so much of their time for taped interviews and the writing up of their experiences. Thank you Matt, Bob, Charlie, Winnie, Madge, Betty, Marie, Josie, Joan, Anne, Marie K., Joan M., Jimmy and Frank. My thanks also to Rosemary, Bill, Lil, Joan, Mr. Higgs (Mayor of Much Wenlock) and Ann Downes (Town Clerk), for providing much information and documentation about the reception and care given to the evacuees from Liverpool. I also want to thank Mrs. Ellen Wright and the staff of St. Joseph's Catholic School, Hednesford, for allowing me to use information from school log-books and registers.

Thanks too to those who contributed their memories of schooldays, and nights in the air-raid shelters, during the period of the Merseyside Blitz: Tommy, Steve, Anthony, Frank and Joan.

My thanks to Pat Ayers and her colleagues from the Docklands History Project, for their support, enthusiasm and practical help. Thanks also to Suzanne Yee and Ian Qualtrough of the Photographic Unit at Liverpool University and to Val Taylor and Sandra Ellams for typesetting and design. I am grateful also to Carl Newell of the Hulton Picture Company for his courteous and prompt response to enquiries.

Finally, I am especially grateful to my husband, Frank, for his unfailing encouragement, interest and assistance.

Joan Boyce
15th May 1989

Frontispiece Liverpool children, bearing gas masks and with their belongings in pillow cases, read evacuation instructions in their school playground.

Introduction

Between September 1st and 6th 1939, a total of 85,000 people were evacuated from Liverpool to various 'safe' destinations as part of the first wave of the government's national wartime evacuation scheme. This was the period of the 'phoney war'. The fear that Britain was under threat of intensive German air raids pressurised many parents into sending their children away. By January 1940, nearly 40% of the Liverpool evacuees had returned to the city.

We can imagine some of the effects this mass exodus must have had upon the parents who were left behind. The loss — however temporary — of their children; the anxiety of knowing that children faced long train journeys to unknown destinations; the knowledge that their children would be handed over to complete strangers; and, of course, the despair brought about by the outbreak of the war itself.

The second wave of wartime evacuation from Merseyside took place shortly after the May blitz in 1941. I was nearly six years old at the time and I was evacuated with four of my older sisters to a seaside town in North Wales - Penmaenmawr.

In Liverpool we lived in a small terrace house in the dockland area of Stanley Road. Our house had three bedrooms, a kitchen, a back kitchen, parlour and basic amenities. In Penmaenmawr we lived in a minor 'stately home' which had many large bedrooms, several bathrooms, huge 'parlours' and extensive gardens bordered by tall trees, through which the sea was always visible. This was the convent of the Seafield Sisters. Once it had been the home of the Owen Owen family, famous throughout Merseyside for their large department store in Clayton Square. With the start of German attacks on Merseyside from August 1940 the 'phoney war' was ended. The reality of death and destruction acted as a spur to parents who quickly took advantage of the second evacuation scheme to remove as many children as possible from the city to areas considered safe from German bombing.

My interest in wartime evacuation is therefore, rooted in my own experience. Memories have remained a source of conversation and nostalgia among friends and relatives who had themselves been evacuees. The convent in Penmaenmawr is still there, although the sisters who looked after us have long since left. These memories and experiences have, in recent years, been given a new dimension through my reading of the social history of the wartime period. From the many sources and accounts of the war, it became evident that the organization and experience of civilian evacuation was unique in British history.

3

A couple of years ago I happened to be visiting Much Wenlock in Shropshire. The visit reminded me that children from my own neighbourhood had been evacuated there during the war. I enquired at the local museum if any official records were held there about the evacuation. I was directed to the office of the Town Clerk, and was given immediate access to a fascinating set of documents which set me on the path to writing this book.

Many people who were evacuated are now well into their fifties and sixties, and they have much to tell about their experiences. With the help of a tape-recorder I have attempted to record some of their memories. My family and friends were generous with their time and provided me with many hours of recordings. North Wales — an obvious choice because of my connections with Penmaenmawr — hosted several thousand children from Merseyside. The choice of Shropshire arose from my visit to Much Wenlock. Staffordshire related to my husband and some of his friends who were sent to Cannock Chase after the May blitz.

This book could not have been written without the close co-operation of these former evacuees. With the help of the questionnaires, taped interviews, and written accounts from individuals, I have been able to reconstruct some of the more significant experiences they remembered. I was also able to interview several people who had acted as 'foster parents' to evacuees. The background and experience of these was rooted in small rural communities and contrasted sharply with the street-wise children they accepted responsibility for. Their views provide several fascinating insights into the complexities of relationships between evacuees and the adults into whose communities the city children had to merge.

Because the wartime evacuation scheme was a unique event in the history of our nation, it follows that the experiences gained by those who participated in the scheme were also unique. I hope therefore, that the accounts of these experiences given in this book, will make a little contribution to our understanding of what happened to ordinary people during the Second World War. I also hope that the book will serve as an encouragement to others to undertake research into the evacuation experience in other geographical locations.

Chapter One

FROM PEACE TO WAR

Before the sirens sounded

The first move towards a national evacuation scheme was taken by the government in 1938, through the setting up of a special committee on *Procedures for Civilian Evacuation*. The Committee submitted its Report to the Home Secretary in July of that year, although it was not published until after the Munich crisis in the autumn. One of the general principles the Committee established was that evacuation would be entirely voluntary. But, it was hoped that through national and local appeals expressed in simple, straightforward language, as many eligible people as possible would be encouraged to participate in the scheme. An order of priorities was stipulated: schoolchildren were to be evacuated first, followed by mothers with children under five years of age, then pregnant mothers. It was expected that some housewives would be persuaded to remain in danger areas 'to provide for the needs of the working population'.[1] The committee assumed that the general public could be relied upon to accept official advice and instructions.

What persuaded the government to devise an evacuation scheme in the first place? Why was it implemented at such an early stage in the war? There were at least two strong reasons. Authorities believed that war with Germany would lead to the massive bombing of our industrial areas. They calculated that up to 600,000 people would be killed, and 1,200,000 injured. This fear was heightened by the prospect that German aircraft would also be used to drop poison gas on British cities. Although these calculations later proved to be excessive, at the time they strongly influenced government planning.

The second reason came from government anxieties over the general level of morale among the civilian population. It was thought that frequent and heavy air attacks could lead to rioting and a breakdown of law and order in industrial regions.

5

The spectre of massive and disorganised departures of people from cities into rural areas was reinforced by newsreels showing similar events taking place in Spain during the civil war; in Abyssinia during Mussolini's campaign there; and in Czechoslovakia, as a result of Hitler's invasion.

Before the Second World War started, civilians in this country were issued with gas-masks, identity-cards and ration books. Anderson and Morrison shelters were built while basements and cellars were reinforced to provide protection during air raids. The evacuation scheme however, was the most far-reaching of the government's plans for wartime Britain, for this was designed to remove millions of civilians, mainly from the vulnerable city areas, in an orderly and peaceful manner, to areas designated as 'safe'.

The first phase of the evacuation scheme was implemented during late August 1939, when war became inevitable, and continued during the early days of September. The Liverpool Corporation, like local authorities in other areas, attempted to persuade as many eligible people as possible to leave the city. Information about the evacuation scheme was distributed through schools, churches, offices, public notices, and official vans fitted with loud speakers.

On Sunday, September 3rd, 1939, the day the Second World War was declared, the parish priest of the Catholic parish of St. Gerard Majella, Cranmer Street, Liverpool, gave his parishioners this message from his pulpit:

> Those mothers who have children under school age and are desirous of evacuating must register if they have not already done so, at the school between the hours of 2 - 4 p.m., today, Sunday for evacuation on Monday. Today is the last opportunity as far as is known for this registration. We are pleased to be able to tell you, on the words of Mr. Tracy, our Headmaster, that all those who were evacuated from school on Friday and yesterday arrived safe and sound and were most hospitably received by the people of Wem (Shropshire).[2]

Similar announcements were made in other churches and no doubt placed parents in a worrying predicament. They were under considerable pressure to send their children away. There were expectations that the German airforce would start bombing attacks on mainland Britain immediately. There was the warning that time was running out for those who were considering evacuation. Betty Mc. then a thirteen-year old parishioner of St. Gerard's, remembered the anguish experienced by her parents:

> The evacuation scheme was supposed to be voluntary yet people were pressurized from all sides: in school, in church, even in the

6

No. 1 *Evacuee children from St. Gerard Majella School. Josie Grimes centre front.*

streets. Father Reilly, the parish priest, warned that it would be the parents' responsibility if children were killed during the bombing. Vans with loudspeakers patrolled up and down the streets shouting : 'Today is your last chance to register. Go to your nearest centre now, before time runs out!' My parents were under great stress, and in the end they decided that it would be best to send us on the evacuation.

The reaction of the parents of Marie, living in Bootle, shows that some parents held a different view:

My mam and dad didn't consider evacuation at all. I was nine when the war began. We used to congregate every night at the top of our street and be taken by lorry to Lydiate. This was supposed to be a safe area. We took our own blankets and we slept on the floor of some church hall, I don't recall the name. It was always packed with people and we were given cups of cocoa and corned beef sandwiches.

Although at the beginning of the war we had air raids and the warning siren went regularly, there was little actual bombing. So we stopped going to Lydiate and we got our own Anderson shelter. Most nights we went to bed fully clothed. When the sirens sounded we just got up and went down the yard and stayed in the shelter until the all-clear sounded.

'We're on our way...'

By mid-September, 57,000 schoolchildren, and 31,000 mothers with children under the age of five, were moved out of Liverpool. The children were all inspected by nurses and given labels to attach to their luggage. They were told to take one change of clothes, soap and toothpaste, and of course, their identity card, ration book and gas-mask. As they lined up to say goodbye to their relatives, they felt a mixture of sadness and excitement.

Matt had clear memories of walking down Silvester Street, Liverpool:

> .... with about forty little children. I had to queue up to have a label tied to my braces and I had to carry my gas-mask over my shoulder. What really sticks is the memory of seeing all the mums standing on the opposite side of the street watching us board the corporation buses, apparently unmoved. I say 'apparently' because, as young as I was, I was very aware of the turmoil and anxiety my poor mum was going through, wondering where her little one was going to sleep that night! I had heard her talking to relatives and neighbours many times about her anxieties. The buses took us to Lime Street Station where we got a train to Nantwich. We were accompanied all the way by our junior school teachers. For me, the evacuation seemed like a great adventure.

For many evacuees — adults as well as children, the 'great adventure' got off to an uncomfortable start! One Liverpool teacher who travelled with a party of children to Shrewsbury recorded 'a corridor train, which stank!' His journey took twelve hours![3] Another non-corridor train carried 400 mothers and children from Liverpool to Pwhelli, North Wales.

Charlie A recalled being one of many children on a long train journey to Aberystwyth. This was followed by a long bus journey to Bronant where they were taken to the village school and met by members of the Women's Voluntary Services. The boys were each given a pair of boots, a woollen jersey, socks and trousers.

For most, the journey meant that it was their first experience of being away from home. The younger children found this exciting, but the older ones were more apprehensive. Some, like Betty Mc., were conscious of new responsibilities:

> I was frightened to death. I had never been away from home before — a trip to town had been something of an adventure! Now, I had the job of looking after three younger sisters, and I was under pressure from my mother and father to make sure that I

No. 2 *Local children assemble at school prior to evacuation.*

No. 3 *Local children board a train to leave the city.*

kept them all together, wherever we were sent. I was only thirteen at the time. However, I felt a bit more secure knowing we were part of a large group of children, all from the same school, and with teachers that we knew.

Marie B. (a younger sister of Betty Mc.) remembered being taken by bus to Lime Street Station where the evacuees were put on a train from Stanton, Shropshire.

The journey seemed very long but we were closely supervised by our teachers. At first, my sister Josie and I thought we were going away on holiday. We were taken into the village hall on arrival, and our teachers stayed with us.

Ann K. confessed that at first, the evacuation was something of a mystery to her — she was eight years old at the outbreak of the war:

I went away on Friday, 1st September with my older brother. At first my parents didn't want us to go, but we pleaded with them to let us, as so many other children in the neighbourhood were going. I didn't understand what 'war' meant. I thought it meant people on one side of the street fighting those on the opposite side! We all had to meet on Rankin's field, our parents came with us, and we couldn't understand why so many of them were crying. I had never been away from Liverpool before, and I remember the train journey that started at Sandhills station and seemed to go on for ever. I couldn't get to our destination quick enough. I thought I was going to live in a big house, all of us together, just like the school girls in the stories in the 'Girls' Crystal'.

On arrival at their destinations, the evacuees were taken to reception centres, usually a village hall, or a school. There they were given some refreshments and a parcel of clothes. Many of the children were also given medical inspections because there was a fear they would be carrying vermin, or suffering from some sickness. As a precaution many of the boys were forced to have their heads shaved, and some of the girls had their hair cut very short.

Betty Mc. remembered that even before she and her sister were allowed into the house, they were taken into a shed in the backgarden where their foster-mother poured paraffin and vinegar onto their hair, and then subjected them to intensive combing, until she was convinced that they were both scrupulously clean. They were then allowed inside the bathroom where they were each given a hot bath and their hair was washed.

11

Ann K. had a similar experience. She shared a billet with three other girls. On arrival a nurse was sent for. The nurse gave them very short haircuts. Ann felt so embarrassed about this that for several weeks she wore a woollen hat to disguise her short hair.

Most of those interviewed retain clear memories of their experiences at the reception centres:

Betty Mc. for example:

> When we arrived in Stanton we were taken to the village hall. I felt like a refugee. I was deeply upset and worried about my sisters. People kept coming in and out of the hall to choose children — it was just like a market! I was determined not to let anyone split up our family, but really it must have been hard for people to take on four girls. Our teachers also tried to keep families together. However we were split up.

Marie B. continues this story:

> It was very frightening waiting in the hall for somebody to come along and choose you! I went with my sister, Nancy, to a family that kept the village post office. Betty and Josie, my other sisters, went with a family that kept a general store. Fortunately the post office and general store were next door to each other.

Local authorities selected as reception areas for evacuees were obliged to appoint Billeting Officers. The role of billeting officer was of considerable importance in the administration of the evacuation scheme. In his satirical novel, *Put Out More Flags*, Evelyn Waugh described the activities of Basil Seal, who poses as a billeting officer in order to blackmail the residents of a village into taking evacuee children from the East End of London.

More seriously, the Borough of Much Wenlock experienced considerable difficulty in keeping their billeting officers, as the Minutes of the Sanitary Committee (1939/41), suggest:

5th October 1939
Mr. Woof tendered his resignation as billeting officer.

2nd November 1939
A letter dated 9th October was received from Mr. Birch stating that he would be pleased to act as billeting officer for Much Wenlock.

2nd June 1940
The Town Clerk reported that Mr. Birch had resigned: ... it was resolved that Councillor Bricknall be appointed in his stead.

12

3rd February 1941
The Council had great difficulty in selecting an officer for the work of billeting officer. Councillor Parslow ultimately undertook to act provisionally.

It is worth mentioning the view of a Liverpool schoolteacher who recorded for Mass Observation:

> I felt sorry for the receiving area or district — the mothers and children are a mixed crowd — black, white, yellow in various degrees, dirty, immoral and quarrelsome and drinking. Pity the poor billeting officer.[4]

One of the responsibilities of the billeting officer was to ensure that accommodation for the evacuees was available and of an adequate standard. Rosemary remembered her own reaction to the evacuation in Much Wenlock:

> People living in the evacuation 'safety areas' were obliged by law to accept evacuees. They had no choice. I remember the day the local officials came to inspect our house. They counted the number of rooms and the number of us who lived in the house. We had one spare bedroom, so we were told we had to take two children. We had to comply. We didn't really want our home invaded by strangers, but we had no option. I suppose we didn't fully realise the seriousness of the situation.

On Friday, September 1st, Rosemary's father went to the reception centre in Much Wenlock:

> It was a shocking sight. About 60 to 70 children were all sitting around inside the Memorial Hall, looking very tired and grubby. They had been travelling a long time. Many of them had been eating sweets and chocolate. Some of them were crying. I have never seen anything so pathetic in my life since. To add to the confusion there was a constant flow of adults coming in and out of the Hall to choose their children.
>
> My father and I eventually took two frightened little girls, Pauline and Stella. We took them home and it was about 9 pm. They had been sitting in the Memorial Hall since 4.30 that afternoon, waiting to be sorted out. I shall never forget the expression of relief on their faces when they arrived at our house.

Lil also lived in Much Wenlock. Her parents had a sweet shop in High Street:

> The evacuees all arrived on Friday afternoon. They were all

13

Catholic children, which surprised us because Much Wenlock was mainly a Church of England area, and we were expecting Church of England children. We found out later that an administrative mistake had been made. The Catholic children should have gone to Madeley, and the children who were sent to Madeley should have come to Much Wenlock! However, the Catholic children brought their own priest - a Father Daley, and their own teachers.

My employer Miss C. took four children, a boy and three girls. She fitted them out with new clothes, but couldn't really cope with them. You see, she had a beautiful home, full of valuable antiques. My parents volunteered to take the boy and Mrs. D. took the girls. The boy stayed with us for two years.

How were the children treated and cared for while they were away? Marie B. said that she and her sister Nancy were kept separate from the rest of the family they lived with:

Our bedroom was very nice but we were given jugs of hot water and bowls for our morning wash. The people were kind, they tried to make us welcome, but we never felt part of the family. We ate breakfast in the kitchen, but we all ate together in the evening. The family thought they were going to make young ladies out of us, and so they tried to teach us table-manners. They were shocked to find that we already behaved well and that we knew our etiquette. I think they assumed that because we came from Liverpool we would be badly behaved and rough.

Josie stayed with the same family as Betty Mc. After about a week they were moved to another family just across the road, Betty explained that Mrs. P. said to her, 'You are old enough to understand. Between looking after the two of you and the store, I can't cope. Mrs. D. is looking for a helper'.

I was very upset at the time, but I just had to do as I was told. Josie and I were moved to Mrs. D's. She had a family of her own, and I was expected to help with the housework as a re-payment to her for taking us in. I never had time to play. I had too much to do in the house. Immediately I came in from school I had to set the table. After the meals I had to wash up. I don't know who did all the cleaning and other jobs before I arrived. If our school uniforms got dirty, I had to wash them. I did a lot of ironing at weekends. We had to keep our bedroom clean and tidy, and Mrs. D. passed us bed linen and showed us where it was kept in an airing cupboard. The housework was heavy. I had to clean and polish a big mahogany sideboard. On top of this were large china figurines that had to be cleaned in every nook and cranny — it was just like the TV series 'Upstairs-Downstairs'. I was the maid. I also had to go to school as well as looking after my younger sister, Josie.

Josie:

> I was put to bed about seven o'clock every evening by Betty, and she then went out for a walk with Miss Wiley, one of our teachers. I wasn't frightened but I never went away from the window until they returned. They were only away for about an hour, but that hour seemed a lifetime to me.

The experience of the evacuation for those who took part in this first phase was short-lived. This can be explained by the circumstances of the early months of the war. Expectations that there would be immediate and widespread bombing attacks on Britain were not realised. Although, as Angus Calder records, 'the threat of bombardment swelled a mighty exodus from the cities ... yet there were no bombs, there was very little war'.[5] In Liverpool, 28% of those who had left the city during September had returned by the beginning of January 1940.

'We're coming home...'

Towards the end of 1939, the University of Liverpool began an inquiry into the effects of the evacuation.[6] A total of 356 families (230 mothers and 1002 children), all living within the city centre and all eligible for the scheme, were taken as a sample. Of these, only 74 mothers and 570 children actually took part in the scheme. What is interesting about this inquiry is that it gives details of destinations, and of problems experienced by families as a consequence of the evacuation.

Destinations

Place	Evacuated	Total away	Still Returned
Anglesey, St. Asaph	94	59	35
Chester	381	188	193
Lancashire, Cheshire	56	28	28
Not known	39	3	36
Totals	570	278	292

No. 4 *Carefree children from Butler Street School photographed in June 1939.*

No. 5 *Butler Street school children evacuated to Leeswood in September 1939.*

Of the 74 mothers who went on the scheme, only 3 remained away at the end of 1939. The large number of children who returned from Chester is explained as being due to lack of suitable accommodation. The strange case of the 39 who had travelled and failed to find out where it was they had been taken to, is explained by the fact that they had made an immediate return to Liverpool. However, 3 children were still in 'unknown' destinations at the end of 1939. The University inquiry also showed that some parents were experiencing psychological and financial problems connected with the evacuation scheme. For example, 42% claimed they were unhappy and worried because their children were away from home. There were complaints of loneliness, and of missing children who had been helpful in running the family home. Financial problems had increased because of the cost of making regular visits to children. Further, there was an obligation on parents to contribute to the maintenance costs of children. Finally, the inquiry made a number of criticisms of the scheme: poor organisation at reception centres; the lack of trained social workers; and the lack of information given to parents about their children.

Some of these criticisms were put into a national context and given a sharper edge by later commentators. Padley and Cole, for example noted the lack of organisation at reception centres because 'many people had started to come back while others were still in the process of going'.[7] A later, more considered view by Calder, highlights some of the social consequences of the first phase of the scheme:

As a disrupted nation settled down to weeks and months when it seemed that almost no Briton anywhere was striking a blow in anger, evacuation dramatized its disunities. It showed how far out of touch was Chamberlain's government with the conditions and opinions of those whom it 'represented'. It exposed the inadequacy of Britain's social services, both in town and country. It offered experimental proof that the poor were hideously poor, in the south-east as well as in Nineteenth-century Britain. It thrust a better standard of living in front of small townschildren, and a far worse one against the noses of middle-class householders.[8]

Many of the issues raised by Calder touch upon the experiences of the evacuees interviewed for the purpose of this book. There were stories of miserly country-people in Cheshire; incomprehensible Welsh people in Llanfairfechan, Prestatyn, Abergele, Colwyn Bay and other places with unpronounceable names. There were memories of teachers billeted in public-houses, and of visits from parish priests anxious to ensure that children were still attending Sunday mass. There were the aches and pains of homesickness,

17

coping with strange food, fights with local kids and arguments between parents. In spite of the novelty of living among green fields, or within sight of the open sea and the mountains, for most, the first phase of the evacuation seemed less enjoyable than life at home among familiar streets and familiar people.

No. 6 *Many children came from very close-knit communities. Rural life could seem strange.*

Betty Mc. now admits that:

> Stanton was a beautiful place but I didn't appreciate it at the time because it was so lonely. Living at home you only had to put your head out of the door and you would meet people. None of the children in Stanton bothered with us. We played with other evacuees, and with the D... children that we lived with.

Matt M. remembered feeling homesick and frightened:

> I looked forward to going to school just to see familiar faces and our own teachers. As a family, we had been split up. Bob and Charlie (my brothers) had been sent to stay at a retired colonel's mansion house. My sister, Winnie, and I were sent to stay with an old Welsh witch in a dilapidated cottage. Although we lived only a couple of miles from each other, Winnie and I missed them very much. I got to the stage of developing sensitive hearing because I could hear Bob's mouth-organ from miles away, playing 'I've Got Sixpence' — top of the Charts at the time! We've often laughed about it since because we seemed to have fish-paste sandwiches for breakfast, dinner and tea, while Bob and Charlie were having the life of Reilly! While they grew fat and prospered, Winnie and I began to show the effects of our fish-paste diet and what I suppose were signs of malnutrition began to become apparent. So much so, that when our mother visited us along with our Aunt Lily (who even the local 'Bobbies' stayed away from), the old 'Welsh witch' was sorted out in good style, and we were promptly whisked home. Bob and Charlie stayed on a bit longer. They were treated like the long lost sons of the retired Colonel in the manor house.

Betty Mc. eventually wrote home to tell her mother that she was homesick:

> I threatened to walk every foot of the road home. Mam wrote back saying 'Give it a fair trial'. After a month, I don't know who it was, but someone came with a car and took us home through the Mersey tunnel.

Josie (her sister) thought it was through the advice of her teacher, that they were eventually brought home:

> Knowing that Betty was being used so much for house-work was a worry. But at home, the expected bombing had not materialised. There didn't seem much point in staying any longer.

Poverty and Health — The Public Debate

One of the reception areas that began to express concern over the effects of the evacuation was Wrexham. We can see from newspaper reports published at the time that the Wrexham authorities grew increasingly critical of the Liverpool City Council on at least two issues: the state of the children's health, and schooling: The *Sunday Pictorial* dated 24th September 1939 reported:

Wrexham Education Committee have passed a severe censure on the Municipal Authorities of Liverpool and Merseyside for allowing children to be sent to the Wrexham area in a 'filthy condition'.

The Report of the Medical Officer for Wrexham, dated September 11th, 1939, shows that out of 800 Liverpool children examined on arrival:

10	had impetigo
14	had bronchitis
49	had tonsil/adenoid problems
2	had scarlet fever
2	had chicken-pox
5	had malnutrition
35%	of girls had head lice
11%	of boys had head lice

The pressure upon local authorities with regard to the provision of suitable and adequate schooling can be seen from a letter published in a Wrexham newspaper from the headmaster of Wrexham Boys' County School. In this he argues that the shift system of schooling which enabled pupils from Calder Girls' School and Quarry Bank Boys' School to use his school premises was proving unsatisfactory, and leading parents and children to ask permission to return home to Liverpool:

If that permission is granted all may be well. If they stay, temporary buildings need to be erected costing £800 for a full timetable, fair play and independence. Liverpool has a duty to perform in looking after its children and up to the present moment nothing has been done beyond sending them to Wrexham as a reception centre and hoping for the best.[9]

The educational and social problems the evacuation scheme revealed made a considerable impact on politicians and social reformers during the war. It highlighted the differences between social groups in the country, a point picked up by Alderman Cyril Jones, of Wrexham, during a debate on the evacuation:

One result of the evacuation had been to make them realise there were two Englands. One was a civilised country, and the other was far below the civilisation that existed in the Wrexham area for many years. These children will be going back to Liverpool when the emergency is over and I only hope that by that time the authorities there will have wakened up.[10]

Oliver Lyttleton, a member of the wartime cabinet from 1941, wrote in his memoirs:

I had little dreamt that English children could be so completely ignorant of the simplest rules of hygiene, and that they would regard the floors and carpets as suitable places upon which to relieve themselves.[11]

No. 7 *Children sometimes came from appalling housing conditions. Burlington Street, 1934.*

The Women's Institutes of England and Wales reported that schools had to be fumigated after the reception of evacuees. Some children suffered from scabies. Clothing was in a deplorable condition, and many mothers and children were bed-wetters.

Reports such as these contributed to some of the mythology surrounding the evacuation. Did the criticisms relate to the majority of children, or only a minority? Did the criticisms act as excuses for people who may have been reluctant to accept evacuees? We shall never produce convincing answers to such questions. However, we do know that the experience of evacuation sank into the consciousness of some political thinkers who used the experience as a means towards reconstructing Britain in the post-war years, especially in educational and social reforms.

The effect of the 'phoney' war — no bombs, and life going on as usual — was a major reason for many returning home, after such a short time on the evacuation. Many parents felt that they had been persuaded to send their children away under false pretences. Some mothers had financial difficulties to cope with: in some cases having to contribute to the maintenance of the children while away from home. Others, as the University researchers discovered, were suffering psychologically because of being separated from their children. Although a few children persevered and stayed on in their new homes and communities, the vast majority were glad to return to their homes. What had been going on in Liverpool while they were away?

Chapter Two

KEEPING THE HOME FIRES BURNING

School

The outbreak of the war created problems for the city's Education Committee. Schools due to re-open after the summer holidays remained closed, partly because of the implementation of the evacuation scheme. Because the scheme was 'voluntary', it was difficult for the authorities to make a preliminary assessment of the numbers of children and parents who would want to be evacuated. It was also necessary to arrange for teachers to travel with their pupils and to transfer to the evacuation area schools. This applied particularly to Catholic schools where Catholic parents were under pressure from their priests to ensure that children continued to receive religious instruction in evacuation schools. This pressure prevailed even during the period of air-attacks on Merseyside. Titmuss in his research on the evacuation noted:

> In Liverpool during the raids of 1940-41 some Catholic priests took the view that children should run the risk of being bombed, rather than receive education at non-Catholic schools.[12]

Presumably this explains one of the reasons why so many Catholic teachers accompanied their pupils on both phases of the evacuation. Many children were not evacuated, and with the schools remaining closed, large numbers of them were free to roam the city's streets unsupervised. This became a matter of some concern to parents, teachers and others. In November 1939, a petition from 'the parents of Liverpool scholars' was submitted to the Education Committee. This received the support of the Merseyside Chamber of Commerce in a letter which drew attention to the annoyance caused by the children to shopkeepers. The frustration felt by teachers was summed up in a diary entry for September 16th, 1939:

> The local Education Committee has been sharply criticised by

parents, because of the neglect of children's training ... I wish someone would decide to send us back to school because my class and the others are surely as worthy of education as those evacuated.[13]

This pressure eventually forced the Education Committee to accept that schools would have to be re-opened. This entailed making adequate provision in accordance with government regulations for air raid precautions. The Committee therefore introduced a scheme for children to receive school instruction at designated houses in local communities. The following announcement given at St. Gerard's church on Sunday, 12th November, shows how the scheme was implemented:

> It is proposed to extend to these dockside parishes the scheme of house schooling in which people lend their rooms if suitable for that purpose. You are asked to volunteer to lend rooms if you feel you can. There is absolutely no compulsion about it, but it might mean some sort of education being given to our children. Make your offers to the clergy of the parish.[14]

Marie K., whose parents decided against evacuation for their children, remembered this period clearly:

> Most schools were closed, but my brother and me went to school on odd days of the week. Not to real school, just a couple of afternoons or mornings in certain people's houses. We had lessons but we didn't do much work. I think it was a token effort to satisfy the demands of parents. Lots of kids just roamed the streets and got into mischief.

Frank also had vivid memories of his schooling during this first phase of the evacuation:

> I had no idea why I didn't go away on the first evacuation. Most of my friends, including an aunt and two cousins who lived two houses away from us, went to Cheshire. Once the effect of the mass exodus from the neighbourhood began to show, those of us who stayed behind began to feel heroic. We were in the front line: in the trenches, ready to defend our patch against Hitler and anybody else who attacked.
>
> We also felt liberated from the hard life of school and its dreaded teachers. School buildings were closed. Several teachers—those who we feared the most—had gone off with the evacuees. The remainder of us went to 'school' only twice a week, one morning and one afternoon, in a house in the neighbourhood. This meant that the teacher couldn't really shout at us — at least,

No. 8 *City children, Tichbourne Terrace, 1935.*

not in a very loud voice. Neither could she cane us—not in front of
the neighbours. And she certainly couldn't throw her inkwell or
blackboard duster at us — habits carefully perfected throughout
her teaching career. Such freedom distanced us from the discipline
and anxieties of school and found expression in the streets
through our play.

The streets were quieter because fewer children were around
and we had more space to play. We got to know each other better,
and increasingly our street games were influenced by the war:
through the things we heard, and through the comics and books
we read. The games were usually excuses for the British to beat the
Germans in dog-fights in the air, or in sea-battles. One side of the
street became the location for the British battle-fleet. The other —
the darker, gloomier side, was for the Germans. At first we made
only rude noises in our battles, thinking we were giving good
imitations of guns firing broadsides, torpedoes on target streaking
towards the enemy, mines exploding as they made contact with
unsuspecting ships. Many vessels on both sides were sunk, but we

picked up survivors from the icy waters of the North Sea — a clearly defined area in the middle of the street.

Later, as we grew more sophisticated in the techniques of battle, the man-made noises were supplemented with home-made missiles: bricks, stones, empty tin-cans, old vegetables rescued from over-filled dustbins. All became ammunition which we hurled rather gently across the street, into each other's territory.

The illusion that the Second World War was being fought by us in our tiny street, didn't last long. As our relatives and friends gradually returned from the evacuation, the street began to fill again with children.

And the bombs came whistling down

Between August 1940 and May 1941 more than 3,800 people were killed on Merseyside, and 3,488 seriously injured, as a result of German bombing. The most destructive raids took place in December 1940 and May 1941, the latter becoming notorious in the memory of those who lived through it as 'the May

No. 9 *Ranelagh Street showing the ruins of Charlotte Street, May 1941.*

blitz'. For eight successive nights from May 1st Merseyside was subject to systematic bombing. In Bootle, nine-tenths of the total number of houses were damaged. The city shopping centre, including the libraries and museum in William Brown Street were badly damaged.

On the outskirts every school and church hall was used to provide nightly accommodation for the thousands who sought refuge from the air-raids. It was due to the May blitz that a second phase of evacuation from Merseyside took place. Whereas parents and children had taken part in the first evacuation partly out of fear that the bombing of the area was imminent, those who took part in the second did so because of the horrendous reality and experience of living through the blitz.

Anthony lived in Kirkdale during the May attacks:

> On the night of May 3rd, 1941, I had ironically been to see a film called 'Torrid Zone' starring James Cagney. At about 11.30 p.m. the air-raid warning sounded, and I went to St. John's Church where I had promised to 'fire watch'. The night became a nightmare of droning bombers, exploding bombs, gunfire and searchlights probing the sky. We were terrified. At about 2 a.m. some incendiary bombs dropped into the church but with a combination of sand and stirrup pump we were able to douse them before too much damage had been done. About 5 a.m. I decided to see how my brother and family were faring nearby. I picked up my way cautiously through a lot of debris until I came to his street where I was met by an eerie silence, and where his house had been, there was nothing but crumbled brickwork. I saw a pair of shoes sticking out and knew they belonged to my brother. I staggered over to nearby Stanley Hospital to try to get some news, and was met by a heart-rending sight. As the beds were all full, people were lying in corridors. A priest from St. John's was going around the dying giving Last Rites, and comforting people. Father Park came over to me and when I explained the situation he went and made a few inquiries and came back with very bad news. My brother was indeed dead, and also his eldest son aged 8. His wife and three more children were all injured but would recover.

Frank recorded some of his memories of the May blitz:

> The worst night of the blitz in our neighbourhood was May 7th. As usual we all sat together in the cellar, lit only by an oil lamp. Our district was devastated by the bombing: houses, factories, churches and schools were destroyed or severely damaged. As the air-raid gathered momentum the noise of the bombing increased.

Blue flashes swept across the tiny, confined space of the cellar at regular intervals. We could smell burning all the time. We could hear buildings collapsing and the sound of ambulances and fire-engines.

When we emerged from the cellar after the 'all-clear' it was difficult to recognise our own street. Houses were windowless, some had had their doors blown off. The church in the next street, a tall steepled building, had been damaged by a land-mine. A balloon-barrage unit in the grounds of the church had been destroyed, and some of the airforce men killed. The smell of burning wood was over-powering. All around us were police, firemen, and air-raid wardens trying to prevent us from going into our own houses, and telling us to move out to an area of safety. But where? How could we find out which areas were safe? Even if we did find some place, how could we get there? There were no trams or buses running because of the damage. Out of the chaos we began to realise that an unexploded bomb lay in the next street to ours. We could see it as we passed by, its fish-like tail angled above the pavement, the rest of it embedded in the ground. We were bombed-out!

No. 10 *Devastation where once there were homes. Surrey Street, Bootle, October 1941.*

During the intensive bombing of Merseyside during May, 1741 people were killed, and 1154 seriously injured. The length of the raids varied from two and a half hours, to over four hours. Nearly 90,000 houses in Liverpool, Bootle and Crosby were damaged or destroyed — 40% of all the houses in the area. What happened to people whose homes were destroyed or damaged during the period of the attacks?

Tommy:

> Being 'bombed out' meant that you couldn't go near your home, so we had to spend each day for about a fortnight visiting relatives and friends. We would leave early each morning, take a tram into town and walk around until dinner time when we would meet other neighbours and relatives in Thorne's Cafe, Scotland Road.

Steve:

> During the emergency brought about by the bombing, arrangements were made to take civilians out to the suburbs every evening. We had to meet in Great Crosshall Street. Then, having been loaded onto army trucks we were taken to Rupert Road School, Roby. There, we were given a mug of tea and a slice of bread, and we went to sleep on the hard floor in one of the classrooms. Finding a space wasn't always easy. We had to do this for about a fortnight.

A letter from an 'eyewitness' published in Bombers over Merseyside:[15]

> At night, lorry after lorry goes down our road (the only one open at all), with men, women and children, with blankets and pillows, etc. They are taking them up into Huyton Woods to sleep — but they are laughing and cheering the whole time — wonderful people.

In spite of this evidence of calm and high spirits, Angus Calder claims that in May 1941, after the eighth successive night of intensive bombing on Merseyside, there was a rumour that Liverpool had been placed under martial law. This rumour, recorded by a member of the Mass Observation team:

> fostered no doubt by the cordon which was placed around Merseyside and the difficulty of getting letters out, was credited in London... by an M.P., by a B.B.C. official, by the editor of an important newspaper, and by a senior officer in the services. Many of the most responsible Liverpool citizens believed that a demonstration for peace had been staged... There was, indeed, more anger on Merseyside than had been elsewhere...[16]

Anthony, recorded above, also remembered the reaction of ordinary people to their ordeal:

> Those nights of bombing and death... clearly affected the people's morale... in some cases white flags had been seen fluttering from windows and there is no doubt in my mind that

No. 11 *Pioneer Corps. at work. May 1941.*

had the raids gone on much longer in their intensity the people themselves would have pressurised the government to surrender. They had taken so much physically and psychologically.

Shelters

Although the prolonged period of bombing brought death and destruction to Merseyside and its people, evenings spent in air-raid shelters often had their lighter side as these reminiscences indicate.

Frank:

> Our shelter developed its own sub-culture which centred around several strong personalities. Most of the women got into the habit of sitting in the shelter at night, even if there was no air-raid. The men who, for one reason or another had not gone away in the forces came into the shelter after the pubs had closed. They would. bring in with them bottles of beer and stout, chips and fish, lemonade and crisps, and these would all be shared out between us. A sing-song would start, and everyone would join in. If the men were particularly drunk one or two of them would start singing crude songs and this would draw down the wrath of Bridget.
>
> Bridget was the mouthpiece of the shelter community. Fiery and fearless, she was the only capitalist in the street for she owned the corner shop. This gave her status and power. She had an ancient parrott, and an ancient uncle called Johnny. Uncle Johnny never came to the shelter, yet his invisible presence came to dominate our nights there. He was a fountain of all knowledge on the progress and conduct of the war. He KNEW when and where the next German attack would take place. He KNEW what Churchill and Roosevelt were saying to each other. Johnny KNEW Hitler personally because they had lived in the same Liverpool street after the first world war. Johnny KNEW that Churchill was a war-monger because he had sent thousands of our lads to their deaths in the Dardenelles during the first lot. Churchill hated Liverpool because he had sent the gun-boats up the Mersey during the General Strike. Johnny also believed that the Royal Family could have put a stop to the war at anytime because they were Germans themselves, and cousins of the Kaiser.
>
> From time to time, Johnny's expert knowledge was supplemented with information from Bridget's 'ginger-beer man'. He delivered the lemonade and soft drinks to her shop every week.

While he was in the shop, he would discuss the latest news from Berlin, broadcast over the wireless by arch-traitor, Lord Haw-Haw (also known personally to Johnny). We listened with growing horror as Bridget listed the streets, shops and buildings in Liverpool, selected for destruction by the Luftwaffe. She was astonished that Churchill was not as well informed about the war as Uncle Johnny. Couldn't something be done to stop the bombers if Johnny knew which way they were coming? But 'they' — government, royal family, generals, admirals, bishops and archbishops, wouldn't take any notice of Uncle Johnny, would they? And so the war would go on and on until we were all killed off. Uncle Johnny believed that multiple deaths of working-class people were what 'they' really wanted. The war was a sham to get unemployment down, clear the slum houses, and so help to make the rich, richer.

Bridget always sat on the only cushioned chair in the shelter. While telling us about Uncle Johnny, she would clutch her rosary-beads tightly. As a diversion from her uncle, she would focus on the children and complain about the noise she said they were making. Her whispered 'Hail Mary's' flowed easily and naturally into a litany of warnings: 'You', her large eyes threatening as she glared at us, 'sit still. The Germans'll hear you if you make a noise'.

During the worst moments of the blitz as the shelter was almost ripped in two by the blast of the bombs, I remember Bridget standing, still saying her rosary as she held her beads in an act of defiance shouting: 'You f... German-headed bastards!' This combination of prayer and profanity has given me an everlasting memory of wartime Liverpool.

Jimmy:

The shelter we used was very badly built. When the raids were on, we used to watch the German aircraft flying overhead through slits in the wall. The conditions inside were shocking. I remember when the workmen came in and dumped a heap of sand in the middle of the floor. They told us this could be used for our toilet.

Betty:

The bombing was a terrible experience, but the neighbourliness and concern that people had for each other was exceptional. Evenings in the shelter, and the memory of people praying and singing is something I shall never forget.

Joan:

> I didn't go to the shelter very often because my mother had two
> very young children and me. We used to make a bed under the
> table in the kitchen. On the night when the Rotunda was bombed
> we were forced to go to the shelter underneath Abe Young's shop
> in Stanley Road. I found this amazing. Families had their own
> areas sectioned off and they had turned them into little kitchens
> just like the ones they had at home. One family had a hammock
> slung across a corner of the shelter. I was convinced that the little
> blonde girl who was asleep in it must have been a princess!

The final memory of shelters reminds us of their vulnerability during the
bombing:

Anthony:

> My dad was a tram driver. He experienced a very sad event which
> had a deep effect on him for the rest of his life. Whenever he was
> driving his tram during a raid he always tried to drop his
> passengers off at a convenient air-raid shelter before driving back

No. 12 *Portrait of the King and Queen salvaged from the ruins of the Protestant Reformer's
Memorial Church, Netherfield Road. May 1941.*

to the depot. During a particularly bad raid he dropped his passengers off at a shelter underneath a school. The next morning, he heard that the school had had a direct hit and everyone in the shelter had perished. There were about 200 people killed. Lots of them had been scalded when water pipes burst.

Pillowslips
and
Gasmasks

Chapter Three

AFTER THE BLITZ...

More Departures... and Arrivals...

The regular bombing of Merseyside between Christmas 1940 and May 1941 encouraged a gradual trickle of people to return to the evacuation areas from January 1941. By the end of May the trickle had developed into an exodus. The May blitz had such a traumatic effect on the Merseyside people, that parents had no hesitation in sending their children away. This point was emphasised by

Marie K.:

> After the May blitz of 1941 things were shocking. Some of our neighbours were killed. Others were injured and bombed out of their homes. Most people were terrified. My mam and dad explained to us in detail about the evacuation and the reasons why it was necessary for us to go away. I felt very frightened, but I wasn't stupid. I knew I had go to. Some of my classmates had been killed.

In January 1941, Marie B. and two of her sisters, Josie and Nancy, were sent to North Wales. This came about because of family circumstances as much as the continuing fear of bomb attacks. Twenty-two relatives of the three sisters were forced to share their parents' small terraced house in the northern docks area of the city. Their grandmother, and two aunts and their families had all been bombed out of their own homes, during the Christmas attacks. The grandmother's house, situated in Athol Street, was very badly damaged. The windows and doors had been blown out, and the children's grandfather, already an invalid, had to be carried down the damaged staircase by an older sister, Madge. She explained that eventually the ambulance men arrived:

> They carried grandad out into the ambulance and took him away.

We heard nothing further for three days. We had no idea where he had been taken. Then they told us he was in Wrightington Hospital — this was miles away from where we lived, and we weren't sure of how we could get there!

The cramped conditions at home eventually forced Marie's parents to send her and her sisters Josie and Nancy, to Penmaenmawr.

Although the first phase of the evacuation scheme has been subject to much discussion by social investigators and historians, the second phase has generated less interest. Therefore, less documentation is available on the numbers that took part, and about the areas the children were sent to. My general impression is that substantial numbers left Merseyside for North Wales, Shropshire, Cheshire, and Staffordshire, and that they tended to stay for longer periods than they had done in the first phase. But this time the evacuees took with them vivid memories of the bombing and destruction. They were glad to get away to areas that promised safety and comparative peace. In some cases families went away together: mother, teenagers and young children. This was encouarged by the fear of further bombing.

North Wales

Josie rembered arriving at Penmaenmawr with her sisters so late at night in January 1941, that the billeting officer had gone off duty. As a temporary measure they were taken with other Liverpool children to the Convent of the Seafield Sisters for an overnight stay. The next day it was decided that the nuns would keep seven of the girls included in the group. Seven of the boys were accommodated in a nearby Franciscan monastery, and the remainder of the children were distributed to families in the town.

After the May blitz the sisters were joined by their mother, older sister Betty Mc. Joan aged five, and a younger brother Harry and a sister, Pat, both under school age. Circumstances at home had deteriorated even more because of the continuation of the bombing.

Betty Mc. explained that the May blitz had caused extensive damage in the neighbourhood. The Rotunda theatre had been destroyed and the church of St. Gerard severely damaged by fire. Her father had helped to dig out the dead and injured from the ruins of the buildings and houses destroyed by the bombing. Some victims could be identified only by clothes and jewellery.

Joan joined her three sisters Marie, Nancy and Josie at the convent, but by May 1941 Betty had left school, and was no longer eligible to be included in the evacuation scheme. Special arrangements had been made in

No. 13 *Surrey Street, Bootle. October 1941.*

Penmaenmawr to billet mothers with children under school age. This enabled their mother to live in a nearby hotel — requisitioned for the purpose with the youngest children. As a concession, the authorities agreed that Betty could live in the hotel with her mother. They stayed at the hotel for six months, by which time, the bombing of Liverpool had ceased. Marie and Nancy stayed at the convent until they became of working age, while Josie and Joan stayed until the end of the war.

Joan retained clear memories of her experiences in Penmaenmawr:

My earliest memories as an evacuee include an awareness of contrasts. At home life was lived out in a community in which everyone lived in similar houses, the children went to the same elementary school. Most of the men were away at the war, or working on the docks or at local factories. The women were at home becoming expert at keeping families together and performing the financial miracles which enabled the children to be dressed decently, well-fed and

37

generally healthy and happy. In Penmaenmawr life was of a different order. There was first of all space. There were the large gardens and neighbouring fields. The sea, sometimes rough and frightening, sometimes blue and enticing, was within five minutes walk. There were the nuns: strict, mysterious in their long flowing habits, fitting city children into the routine of convent life. This meant frequent church attendance and regular prayers. It meant that the slightest hint of bad behaviour from us was frowned upon. But it also meant other things like the smell of polish on the convent floors, wood-panelled walls, birds singing in the trees, fresh fruit at meal times, and flowers, newly cut, placed carefully in large colourful vases in every room. The peace and serenity of community life in the convent must have been rudely shattered by the rough and tumble of children from dockland Liverpool. But the security of belonging as a child to a tightly-knit, working-class community was also shattered by the bombing of Merseyside which brought deaths and devastation to the area.

Joan, Josie and Marie were always aware that they were fortunate in having accommodation which was very comfortable and pleasant as well as offering security in troubled times. Other children in Penmaenmawr were not so fortunate. Many called to the convent regularly and the nuns provided them with extra food because some children were under-fed. Marie recalled several children who were put into other accommodation which caused them distress. One boy who wet the bed because he was nervous and frightened, had to endure the embarrassment of having his mattress placed in the front garden of his billet for all his school friends to see, as they passed the house on their way to school. She remembered another boy who, with his younger brother, ran away because they were unhappy. They tried to reach home, but when they arrived at Edge Hill, Liverpool, they were picked up by the police and returned to Penmaenmawr. Their parents were not informed of this event until several weeks later. The girls were expected to help with the cleaning in the convent at week-ends, and the nuns exercised strict control over times for going to bed. They did not like the girls to mix with the boys billeted at the monastery. On the odd occasion when individual girls stayed out later than they should (8 p.m.!), they were locked out of the convent, just to teach them a lesson. They were allowed in, of course, after a short period of anxiety!

Winnie and Matt:

> The area where we lived was badly damaged and an unexploded bomb had landed outside our aunt's chip-shop in Vescock Street. This was the deciding factor for the whole extended family to

organise themselves, and get away to a safer area.

The local coal merchant offered his services and took thirty-two of our relatives down to Lime Street station on the back of one of his lorries. The station was crowded with people, all trying to evacuate. There were so many of us that the Station Master had to add an extra coach on to the North Wales train just for us!

Charlie (a bother of Matt and Winnie) recalled the journey:

The train travelled very slowly and stopped at every station when we arrived in North Wales. When it pulled in to each station, officials would be waiting and would come over to meet our officials. They shouted out the number of evacuees they could accept — 'No more than twenty...' 'No more than ten...' Sometimes they couldn't take any at all, so they would signal to the driver of the train to carry on to the next station. It was just like selling cattle at a market. Eventually, our family reached Abergele and we got fixed up there.

This was very late in the evening. Matt and Winnie continue:

There were no officials at Abergele to attend to us. The local vicar opened up the parish hall. He allowed us to stay until we were fixed up by the billeting officer the following day. It turned out to be one of the funniest nights we had ever experienced.

Local people generously came to our assistance with blankets and items of food. The men in our group organised one section of the hall as a sleeping area, and all the women organised a meal. The numbers to be catered for were many and this posed a problem for the cooks. One of our aunts came up with a bright idea. She acquired two white enamel buckets from God knows where! With help from the other women she proceeded to prepare an enormous amount of stew (scouse). This was enjoyed by all, including the friendly vicar. Before going to bed, we all joined together for a raucus sing-song!

The next day, the billeting officer arranged to take us to a small village called Pensarn. We were given the option of renting a large boarding house which had been requisitioned for evacuation purposes. We were all happy to take advantage of this offer, and so we moved in. We stayed in Pensarn for about fourteen months. Many of the grown-ups got work in the local leather factory. Most of them returned to Liverpool at the end of the summer of 1942.

For the whole of the second phase of the evacuation, Winnie and Matt were very happy and contented. They enjoyed living close to the seaside very much.

Everybody seemed to get on well together. Neither of them remember there being any conflict between the evacuees and local people. Despite the excitement and happiness of their stay in Pensarn, they were pleased to return to Liverpool and to settle down once again to a normal family life.

Joan M. lived at the outbreak of the war in a small terraced house in Liverpool 7, with her mother, baby brother, and grandfather. Her father was serving abroad with the army.

After the heavy bombing in May 1941, Joan's mother took advantage of the evacuation scheme, and they moved to Gronant in North Wales. There they lived in a tiny cottage rented from the local postmistress. The cottage consisted of two rooms, a bedroom and a living/kitchen area. Outside they had a chemical toilet. There was only one double bed which Joan shared with her mother and baby brother.

Joan was not impressed with Gronant when she first arrived, it looked bleak and lonely. But, after a short time she began to enjoy the wide open spaces and the freedom of the beach. She remembered the long pleasant walks through the woods and the countryside that she shared with her family. She

No. 14 *Teachers and pupils from Notre Dame High School photographed 'somewhere in Glamorgan', September 1939.*

began to feel contented and secure. When her brother was old enough to start school, her mother got a job in an aircraft factory in Rhyl.

Early in 1944 a letter received from the War Office informed them that her father had been taken prisoner by the Germans. A month later they received a further letter informing them that he had been released and was on his way home. Excited and happy they returned to Liverpool to await his arrival. Tragedy struck. The ship Joan's father was travelling on was torpedoed and he was drowned. Joan admits to retaining many happy memories of her stay in Gronant, but she continues to feel very bitter about the war because of the sadness it caused to her family. Her mother was forced to work for the rest of her life because of the paltry war widow's pension she received from the government.

Shropshire

One of the areas Liverpool children were sent to for both phases of the evacuation was Much Wenlock. The Minute Book for the Borough (1928-1944) includes comments on the reception of evacuees in May 1941:

> That in view of a possible sudden evacuation the Council make application for a supply of boots and clothing (provided by the American Red Cross and other bodies solely for evacuees) to be stored at some convenient centre in the Borough.
>
> E.E. Bennett (Mayor, 20th May 1941).

Later, the following is recorded:

> The Town Clerk reported that 1,877 had been received from Liverpool... when it was resolved —
>
> (a) That the best thanks of the Council be tendered to the reception and billeting officers, and also to the residents of the Borough for the splendid reception they had given the evacuees.
>
> (b) That the Ministry be informed that the Borough was not at present capable of accommodating further evacuees.
>
> The Town Clerk also reported that it had been necessary to incur a certain amount of expenditure on evacuation... when it was resolved that an evacuation account be opened by the transfer of one hundred pounds from the Borough fund thereto... The Council expressed their displeasure and surprise at the condition in which some of the children had been evacuated.

Commenting on the last point, Lil, a resident who had had experience of the first phase of the evacuation, recalled that some of the children arrived in a deplorable state for the second phase:

> Some had been virtually bombed out of their homes and lost all their belongings. It was a shocking sight. The children were filthy. Some had even lost members of their families. It was really very sad. It was only then that people began to fully realise the full extent and seriousness of the situation in Liverpool.

Longmate, in his study of wartime Britain, *How We Lived Then*, helps to illuminate this situation with his comments on evacuee children:

> The most widespread problem of all was providing evacuees with proper footwear... innumerable evacuees arrived with cracked and broken shoes quite inadequate for country roads — Liverpool, the subject of so many critical stories, earning the name of 'plimsoll city'.[17]

Lil believed that Liverpool children were poorer than the children of Much Wenlock. One reason was that Liverpool families tended to be larger. The other reason was that Wenlock people tended to be better managers of their money. She gave the example of her own family where her mother not only ran a local shop, but also took in washing, and grew most of her own vegetables.

One of the Liverpool evacuees sent to Much Wenlock was Jimmy. He came from the dockland area of north Liverpool known as 'over the bridge'. In the May blitz Jimmy's neighbourhood had been extensively damaged. Jimmy recalled the night before he left home to travel to Wenlock:

> My mother worked very hard to prepare my clothes, making sure that my best suit would be ready for the journey. That night, there was another air-raid. While we were in the shelter, our house was bombed, and all our clothes, including my evacuation suit were destroyed. I had to travel in the only clothes I had — a tatty shirt and a pair of trousers.

Jimmy travelled to Much Wenlock with his brother:

> All the children had to assemble in St. Alban's school hall. We weren't sure what was happening, or what the commotion was about. We were given an apple and an orange each. We had to carry our gas masks and ear-plugs. I felt excited, but I couldn't understand why, or why so many parents were crying. Eventually we were taken to Sandhills station, then on to Much Wenlock with children and teachers from our school.

No. 15 *Mr. Hughes' class evacuated from St. Alban's school to Much Wenlock.*

On arrival they were taken to a reception hall where, again the officials and foster-parents of Much Wenlock had gathered to meet the evacuees from Liverpool. Jimmy and his brother were sent to a house which accommodated twenty-three evacuees. It was difficult for him to settle down because the woman who ran the house was nasty to all the children. She was strict and allowed little freedom for play and normal childhood activities.

The quality of the food was poor and there wasn't much of it. He had to share his bed with two other children, but as this had been the case at home he didn't find this much of a burden. Jimmy's parents visited their children regularly. They quickly realised that their children were not happy because of the lack of good food, but they felt there was nothing they could really do about it, except to take food parcels when they visited Much Wenlock. Jimmy and his brother used to hide this extra food away from the other children in the house, and make it last throughout the week.

Lil recalled:

> I found it hard to understand some of the behaviour of the children. Their taste in food was totally different from my own. They didn't care very much for fresh vegetables. They used to call green-beans 'grass'. Their favourite food was always fish and chips.

Jimmy's father was active in the trade union movement. At weekends he would visit Wenlock with a group of other parents. Often, the adults would go drinking in the local pubs. Afterwards they would stand around together in the market-place. Jimmy explained that his father needed no encouragement to spark off a political discussion, often in a loud and aggressive voice. Sometimes this drew the attention of the local police:

> *5th June 1941.*
> A general complaint was made with regard to the conduct of evacuees and their parents particularly the latter, and the Town Clerk was instructed to draw the attention of the police to the matter.

(Much Wenlock Sanitary Committee Book, 1938/42)

In a later statement, dated 1st January 1942, reference is made to continuing bouts of hooliganism in the town centre.

Lil recalled that when visiting their children, Liverpool parents would sit around the clock-tower in the town square. It wasn't unusual to see mothers breast-feeding their babies. Such a public display was frowned upon by the Wenlock people.

Jimmy remembered some of the aggression between Wenlock children and the evacuees:

> We shared the same school as the Wenlock children but we used to have religious instruction from the priest at 10.30 every morning. On the way home from school we often had gang fights. Eventually, the priest told us to stop it, and so we just walked away when trouble started. The Wenlock kids used to mock us for this, but we couldn't go against the priest — he ruled! When we'd settled down we used to get involved in tough games and bad behaviour. We'd have competitions with local kids about who could throw the furthest. Then we'd get old tyres and get inside them and roll downhill. We'd dare each other, like on one occasion I got inside an old pram and rolled down the hill. It was a miracle I didn't break my arm!

Rosemary thought that the evacuees brought about many changes in Much Wenlock:

> It was no longer the peaceful little place they had all been used to. The children were unfamiliar with the countryside. Many had never seen pigs and cows before. I remember a group of small boys trying to ride on the backs of some pigs, and causing havoc in the high street.

44

No. 16 *People in the reception areas were sometimes bewildered by the behaviour of city children.*

Lil remembered that:

> Many of the evacuee children found jobs like delivering groceries and newspapers. There was some pilfering, but nothing too serious. One evacuee told me that back home in Liverpool, children would steal apples and sugar from wagons on the dock road. I used to think that pilfering was part of their normal behaviour. I think the evacuation brought so many different opportunities for children from the cities. The experience made them much better people.

Jimmy paid tribute to the care and attention given to the evacuees by their teachers:

> Our teachers were great. We couldn't have survived without them. As a special treat they would take us on a long walk on the hill, and give us lemonade, a cob, and a bun.

Lil recalled the arrival of the American servicemen in the area:

> They caused some trouble with disturbances, but they were good to the children — they used to give them sweets and gum.

Jimmy had a particular memory of the Americans:

The Yanks loved the evacuees, and they gave us lots of sweets and gum. I made a mate of one particular American called Jake. One

```
                                        . . . . . . . . . eet,

                                        PENZANCE.

                                        25th June, 1945

Dear  . . . . . . . .

        Now that the time is fast arriving when we must
bid adieu to you all, I feel that I cannot allow the
occasion to pass without tendering my warm appreciation
for all that you have done during your sojourn with us.

        I would háve liked to have sent each of you a
personal letter but my sentiments are none the less
sincere even though they take the form of a circular.

        Those of you who came in 1940 need no reminder
of the appaling  conditions in which you worked and
that you bore with our mistakes and shortcomings
with such cheerfulness, has gained our great respect.

        That evacuation has been so largely successful
has in no small measure been due to your unstinted
and devoted service to the children in your care.

        The manner in which you have accepted our mode
of life and thrown yourselves whole heartedly into
the social life of the community is I know, greatly
appreciated and has assisted in keeping civilian morale
to the high level maintained during the war.

        One does not forget that many of you will be
returning to shattered homes,blitzed schools, large
classes and overcrowded conditions.

        It is my earnest wish that your future will be a
happy one and that "the best is yet to be", and that
you will always have happy memories of your stay in
Cornwall.

        I would only add that, should you ever decide to
re-visit this area on holiday you will receive a warm
welcome.
                        Yours very sincerely,

                        . . . . . . . .
```

No. 17 *Teachers who accompanied children took on an enormous responsibility for their physical and emotional welfare.*

46

night I ran away from Mrs. J. (our foster-mother) and went to the American base. I got inside a tent which was full of cartons. Being the lad I was I just had to open a carton, and I could see that it was full of bars of chocolate. So I ate and ate. Gradually I started to get pains in my stomach and I started to cry, 'I want Jake, I want Jake'. Jake was found, and came to see me. He called me a lot of rude names and explained that what I had eaten wasn't chocolate but laxative! He ran me back to Mrs. J's in a jeep. I was in such a mess by that time that she just threw me under the pump and washed me down. I was sick for days!

Marie K. remembered that one particular boy didn't have a very pleasant time. He was billeted with a woman who often left him and his younger brother locked out of the house for long periods. Consequently, he used to get into a lot of trouble. Most people were sympathetic towards him because they were aware of his situation.

On occasions when we went to the pictures as a special treat, sometimes the film would break down. This boy used to get up on the stage and sing. He would make everyone join in the chorus. He had such a lovely voice.

Jimmy remembers the same boy singing outside the local cake shop for a 'penny tart'. He attracted many customers!

Richard Pooley in his book *The Evacuee*, tells of a similar situation which helps us to gain an insight into the experience of Marie. K's friend:

She told us to go out and not come back until nine-o-clock... As it got dark and cold we all piled into the outside lavatory... Charlie whimpered with the cold and I cuddled him like my mother... Ten-o-clock came and went before we heard the bolt being drawn back... stiffly we followed her into the kitchen where we were told to get to bed quickly.[18]

The experience of the evacuees as entertainers was something shared by Ann:

One of my most vivid memories was singing for the American soldiers in concerts organised by the local people. The soldiers showed great affection for the evacuees. They kept us well supplied with sweets and other treats. I also had another memorable experience when the film company arrived in Much Wenlock to make the film of *Gone to Earth*. The stars were Jennifer Jones and Esmond Knight. I played the part of an 'extra' — a great thrill for me. When I told my parents and relations at home, they all thought I was going to reach the heights of Hollywood stardom! Whenever I watch the film now on TV, everything comes back to me.

Staffordshire

Frank, who was evacuated to Hednesford, Staffordshire, recalled leaving Liverpool after the May blitz:

On the station at Lime Street the evacuees were in various stages of excitement. Our belongings were in suitcases and pillow-slips, labelled with our names and destinations. The label on my case told me that I was destined for Hednesford, near Cannock, Staffordshire. This was the first time I'd heard of such a place. The crowded platform slowly disappeared from view as the train began its journey.

It was a train without corridors, and in the compartment were six children and Miss M. Miss M's presence terrified me. By reputation she was the teacher most feared throughout the school. Her physical appearance was equally unnerving for she looked every inch like the wicked witch in *The Wizard of Oz*. If I had been given any real choice between Liverpool and the bombs, or Miss M. and Hednesford, I would have opted for the bombs!

During the journey we were made to eat our sandwiches slowly and carefully, and to drink our milk a third of a bottle at a time. Spacing out our food and drink in this manner would prevent us from feeling hungry, and would reduce the need for the toilet — or so Miss M. warned us! Perhaps a sensible decision because the train didn't have toilet facilities.

I noticed the names of railway stations as we slowly passed through: Crewe, Stafford, Rugeley, now all so familiar but then merely names on a railway line. In spite of my fears about her, Miss M. spent time explaining to us some of the interesting features we could see out of train windows: farms, factories, rivers, canals, hills and different types of buildings. She kept our interest until we arrived in Hednesford.

Frank recalled that the train arrived late in the afternoon:

It was raining heavily. Carrying my suitcase and pillow-slip I was hustled into a waiting car and was quickly joined by three other children and a teacher, Miss S., from our local girls' school. There was also a man who wore a trilby and had a deep dimple at the

48

point of his chin. I found out later that he was the billeting officer. I remember Miss S. complaining about the rain and saying 'I have come all this way without my mackintosh. Of course before clothing coupons, one could walk into a shop and buy a mackintosh on a day like this'.

No. 18 *Reception Centre, West Hill School, Hednesford.*

The evacuees were taken to the reception centre, close to the railway station:

> The reception centre was a school — West Hill school. We were led into the assembly hall. This was very crowded, mainly with children like myself, but there were also groups of grown-ups all chatting and looking at us with curiosity. We stacked our belongings neatly together. The labels showing our names and destination were still pinned to our coats. Our faces must have shown our feelings of anxiety and fear. Over tea and biscuits much discussion was taking place between the man with the dimple and adults. Gradually children in ones and twos were led away quietly carrying their belongings, by some of the women. When the hall had almost emptied, Mr. Billeting Officer came over to me and another boy, John, who was waiting, and told us to follow him

outside. We were put into the car that had brought us from the railway station. We were on our way to our billet. That journey was soon to become familiar: past a colliery with its pit-head machinery and sprawling mountain of coal-waste; through a network of narrow streets of houses, some old and neglected, others new and well cared-for, to the end of a lane which led to open fields and the countryside. Ours was the last in a row of about five similar houses, all surrounded by trees and gardens.

Living with a new family:

The first evening with our new family ran to a formula set by the

No. 19 *Frank and John evacuated to Hednesford.*

billeting officer on our arrival at the house: A meal, bath, and letter home saying: 'Dear Mam, I have arrived safely and I am staying with a good family, Mr. and Mrs. B., their address is . . . Love . . .' then to bed!

From my bedroom window on that first night I looked out across the fields and wondered if I was looking towards Liverpool. What was happening there? More bombs?

We stayed with the B. family for about a month then John and I were split up. I went to Mrs. W. a sister of Mrs. B. Before returning to Liverpool in May 1942, I had gone back to Mrs. B. I don't remember the reasons for this triple change of billet.

On our first outing with Mrs. B. we were taken to Cannock — a four mile bus journey — to have our ration books amended. Mrs. B. explained to us that Mr. B. was a baker, and this meant that he worked very hard, usually at night time, baking bread for deliveries the next day. Therefore he had to sleep during the day, and we would have to keep very quiet while we were in the house when he was in bed.

Returning from Cannock we then had to register for school. For this we had to meet in the Catholic parish church — a tall white building in spacious grounds. The weather must have been sunny because children were grouped together sitting on the grass. There seemed to be a large number of children and I recognised very few of them. We were called into the church by a nun and made to kneel down and recite the rosary together. Mrs. B. gave her account of this when she got home that evening. She told her family: 'They all sat in the benches doing this' (here she gave a wrong interpretation of the making of the sign of the cross) 'and kept on saying over and over again the name of Mary. I've never seen anything like it before. It wasn't like a service at all. And those strange nuns were there, all over the church checking up on the children'.

I was mystified by this because she didn't seem to have understood what was going on in the church. I began to realise that Mrs. B. and her family were not Catholics. I think up to then I had believed that everyone was a Catholic. I was very confused.

School:

The school was at the top of a hill in an area mixed with old and new housing, and the start of a long country lane that wound its way back into the centre of town. For many of us that became our favourite walk. Nearby was Hednesford common, an extensive area of open country which cut across several hills from the top of which we could view the country for miles around. Later, as we grew into the ways of Hednesford and its people, the common became the place where differences between local children and the evacuees were settled.

St. Joseph's School, Hill Top, was a Catholic elementary school staffed partly by nuns, for children aged between five and fourteen. Most of the Liverpool children were aged between eight and ten. There were two women teachers from our own school — we all sighed with relief when we were told that Miss M. had returned to Liverpool. There were no concessions from the staff towards evacuees. Much was expected of us because we were Catholics from the big city. We were expected to set high standards of conduct and religious behaviour for the local children, many of whom were not Catholic although they attended the school because it was the nearest one available. The staff — especially the nuns — applied rigorous methods of teaching just like the school at home. Punishment was swift, for careless and untidy work. There was an emphasis on cleanliness. Being smartly turned out with well polished shoes, and hair clean and neatly parted, were taken as signs of religious virtue.

There was an element of competition between the local children and ourselves in our work in the classroom, looking after the school flower-beds and gardens, sport, and celebrations such as those for St. Patrick's day (all the nuns were Irish).

Sunday evenings at 'home':
Sunday evenings were special occasions in both families I lived with. Because they were closely related there was a lot of interchange. Even before I had moved into the home of the W. family I had visited them with Mrs. B. Sunday evenings were always musical evenings when the W's would entertain their friends and relatives. The daughter, M., was an excellent pianist who specialised in light classical pieces such as 'Rustle of Spring'. Uncles and aunts, all members of various church choirs would sing solos or in unison. After I moved into the W. household I was expected to help prepare and distribute the refreshments. One evening somebody had the idea of getting me to sing. After much persuasion I sang 'I'll Walk Beside You'. I can't ever remember learning the words or the music beforehand, but it became my song, a set piece for subsequent Sunday evenings.

The Town:

The town of Hednesford was less interesting for me than its surrounding countryside. It consisted of one main street which included most of the shops, and two busy roads: one leading to Cannock and the other to Rugeley. There were two cinemas, very popular with us, and a spacious park with swings. There was a library in a small building full of old and tatty books. The park and the swings gave the Liverpool children an opportunity to meet and play together. We'd compare how we were being treated by our foster parents, news from home, what sort of food we were getting, pocket money, and swop comics and books with each other. We'd try to imitate the Hednesford accent and manner of speech. It was a quiet town with the people friendly and hospitable. Walking the two miles to school every day made us fit, and toughened us up. It gave us an opportunity to learn the district thoroughly: its streets and shops particularly. Sometimes we would vary our route to school to have a look at less familiar places. One of my favourite shops was called Poyntons, a sweet shop near the railway station. On Friday afternoons after school we would crowd in to buy our sweets. Mr. Poynton, a small fat man made his own sweets and they were very popular throughout

No. 20 *Playing fields, Hednesford, where Liverpool evacuees would meet and play together.*

53

the town. Hednesford's streets and buildings were not spectacular
or memorable. If anything, it was a rather untidy place that had
grown around the south Staffordshire coalfield. The collieries
dominated the landscape, visible wherever you went.

Returning Home . . .

Betty Mc. returned from Penmaenmawr with her mother, Pat and Harry. The
family were missing their father very much, and as life had quietened down in
Liverpool there didn't seem to be any reason for staying away. This was just
before Christmas 1941. Her sisters, Nancy and Marie stayed on at the Seafield
Convent until they became eligible for employment. Her younger sisters Josie
and Joan stayed until the end of the war.

Betty Mc.

> I found the contrast of the conditions between Liverpool and
> Penmaenmawr quite startling. Penmaenmawr was quiet and
> beautiful. Liverpool was in a terrible mess because of the
> bombing. Whole areas had been flattened. It was difficult to
> recognise particular streets. Old familiar shops and buildings were
> missing. Transport was difficult. Water was restricted in some
> districts.

Marie K. returned from Much Wenlock to Liverpool early in 1942.

> I didn't really want to come home. Things had started to settle.
> The bombing seemed to have finished. But also my parents found
> it increasingly difficult to repay the authorities with a share of the
> cost of my evacuee maintenance, which was costing them around
> seventeen shillings per week for me and my brother Joe.

Ann would have liked to have stayed in Much Wenlock:

> I feel I'd have had a better chance to do well in Much Wenlock. I'd
> have had a more wealthy and affluent life. Life in Wenlock was far
> less harsh than in Liverpool. I had to return to Liverpool because
> there was a domestic problem. This was in 1947 — two years after
> the end of the war. I got a job in Tate and Lyle's sugar refinery.
> The other workers skitted my country accent. But my own family
> were proud of me because they thought I talked 'posh'.

Jimmy still lives in Much Wenlock:

> Towards the end of the war my mum and dad came to live in Much
> Wenlock. They rented two rooms and we moved in with them. My
> father eventually got a job in the power station. We all felt that

54

No. 21 *Liverpool children have clubhouse for school. Upton-by-Chester Golf Club, October 1939.*

Wenlock was heaven. When we went back to Liverpool to visit my gran, we found it was in a terrible mess. We were always glad to get back to Wenlock. My first job was as a gardener's boy on Wenlock Abbey estate. My dad, being a trade unionist, thought I was being under-paid, and he made me leave the job. When the war came to an end, the evacuees began to leave. I stayed on and have settled in Wenlock. I'll never leave.

Frank returned from Hednesford in May 1942:

I came home for what was supposed to be a holiday. Relations and neighbours noticed that I'd grown taller, and that my accent had changed. The streets seemed the same. The houses had been patched up. Hednesford had made everything seem smaller. Back in Liverpool everything was on a larger scale. Back home I felt quite settled, and when the time came for me to return to Hednesford I didn't want to go. My evacuation was ended.

Chapter Four

RELIGION AND THE EVACUATION

One of the recurrent themes that emerged during my research on evacuation was religion. In every case the former evacuees were Catholics who had retained memories of incidents or experiences connected with their faith. Sometimes this connection had to do with schooling, or a priest, or with the attitudes towards Catholicism held by people in reception areas. I have already noted the research of Titmuss where, he claimed, some Liverpool priests urged parents to risk the consequences of the bombing, rather than deprive their children of a Catholic education.

Padley and Cole reported one Catholic priest who:

> felt it necessary to call upon the parents of the evacuees to insist upon their return home, alleging that any physical danger they might incur thereby was trifling when compared with the spiritual dangers they ran by remaining.[19]

The priest was addressing himself specifically to parents whose children had been sent to rural Wales where Catholic churches and Catholic schools were few and far between.

Jackson in his study of the evacuation, *Who Will Take our Children?* shows that the Catholic hierarchy raised numerous objections against the 'indiscriminate' placement of Catholic children. He also gives the example of a Liverpool priest, Father Doyle of Holy Cross parish who —

> reportedly disliked the situation for Catholics — especially Menai Bridge — so much so that he went there himself, and ultimately scuttled the whole programme by urging the government to re-evacuate.[20]

Rosemary, the daughter of one of the host families in Much Wenlock recalled the Catholic priest complaining that some of the foster parents were taking Catholic children to Church of England services, and that this could not be tolerated. He approached her family because they took one of their evacuees to the Anglican parish church for afternoon service.

Rosemary explained:

> I took Pauline with me to our church service. It was held at three o'clock in the afternoon because of the blackout. If I had not taken her, Pauline would have had to stay in the house by herself. My parents would not have allowed that. The priest came and raised merry hell about this. I said if he thought I was prepared to miss going to my church just because of minding Pauline, he had another think coming! We told him that Pauline was in our care, not his... On the other hand, Pauline went to mass through hail, rain and snow. She daren't miss. It was just like living in Ireland!

Ann, like Pauline, never missed going to mass when she lived at home, and she was determined to continue to go at Much Wenlock.

> I told an old man who lived in the village about my worry over mass, and he promised to take me on Sunday mornings. I went with him for about three weeks, but I didn't realise that he wasn't taking me to mass, but to a service at the Methodist church. I wondered why the priest wasn't giving us Holy Communion! But when schooling was sorted out, we were able to have mass in a schoolroom every Sunday.

Marie K:

> Some children had to go to church with their foster families. Others had to go to mass, then to church with their foster families.

Frank:

> Religion played an important part during my stay at Hednesford. The nuns thought that the faith of the Liverpool children was in danger because most of them lived with families who were not Catholic. The evacuees were packed into the school and parish choirs and the boys made to serve on the altar. In this way the nuns exercised more control over our lives. The altar boys were obliged to attend church every day and frequently for evening benediction. The members of the choir had regular practices in the church, and had to attend services on at least three occasions each week. The nuns also had a spacious convent adjacent to the church. The altar boys served mass there regularly, and were treated to a huge breakfast of cornflakes, bacon and eggs, and lots of hot toast and marmalade.

58

St. Patrick's Day was the occasion when the nuns wore shamrock carefully pinned to the shoulder of their habits. The children assembled together in the parish church for mass, during which we sang 'Hail Glorious St. Patrick dear saint of our isle'. I had been taught this hymn at my own school in Liverpool, and singing it in a strange church in a strange town, surrounded by strangers made me feel homesick.

Of the two families I stayed with, one, the W's were all church-goers. Mr. W. went to the Anglican, Mrs. W. to the Methodist, and their daughter M., went to the Congregationalist. If you add to this variety of religions, my own Catholicism, the household had a truly ecumenical spirit long before ecumenism became trendy among Christian denominations. Nevertheless, I was sometimes made aware of the oddness of my own religion. Mr. W. thought it a scandal that I had to go to church so early on weekdays. This was because, as an altar boy, I had to take my turn to serve the 7.30 am mass. He believed the parish priest should have been reported to the authorities for making young children get up so early, hail, rain or snow, just to take part in a form of religious mumbo-jumbo! This unwavering faith enabled me on one occasion to stare a Methodist minister directly in the eyes when he visited the W. family. When he asked me who I was, I replied 'I AM A ROMAN CATHOLIC!', and I walked away from him!

Pillowslips
and
Gasmasks

Chapter Five

EVACUATION... SOME LASTING EFFECTS

What effects did the experience of being an evacuee have in the long term? Winnie, who had been evacuated twice — to Cheshire and to North Wales:

> I'm sure and very aware that no one, whatever race, colour or creed, should ever have to face war again. Although we were brought up in a socially deprived area where we didn't see a green field from one year to the next, and was sent off to the peace and beauty of the countryside, I think the majority of evacuees just wanted to be home with those they loved regardless of the danger they had to face.

Joan M. who had been evacuated to Gronant:

> I enjoyed living in Gronant very much. The only sadness was that I knew I would never see my dad again, who I loved very dearly. As a child of thirteen, the only bitterness that I felt about the war was that it had taken my dad away from us. My mum had lost the man that she loved and was left a war widow. This meant that she had to work right up to the time when her health would not allow her to work any more.

Josie reflecting on her time in Penmaenmawr:

> The evacuation was an adventure for us at the time. But it was an horrific time for our parents, who were forced to part with us. It seemed to bring the best out in people. It showed an extraordinary strength of character and a true sense of community spirit.

Betty Mc. (Josie's older sister):

> At Penmaenmawr we enjoyed a sense of freedom and quiet. War is unnecessary and pathetic. They say that war helped with unemployment: what nonsense. Many women who worked

during the war on munitions still suffer from inhaling chemicals that turned the colour of their skin yellow. This country seems to have lagged far behind most of the other countries that were involved. Some of them are much better off economically than us. War served no purpose whatsoever. Who won? No one! If it happened again today, I would hope that my two sons would be conscientious objectors. One effect of the bombing has remained with me. Whenever we have thunder storms, they terrify me, and bring back all the horrors of the war and the bombing. I often go under the table now during thunder storms. Just like I did during the raids.

No. 22 *V.E. Day party in Empire Street. Note the freshly whitewashed surface air raid shelter to the right of the picture.*

Ann:

I enjoyed living in Much Wenlock very much. Being sent away from home didn't do me any harm. It showed me two sides of life — the 'haves' and the 'have nots'. The people of Wenlock seemed to have more material wealth than those we knew in Liverpool. But they were careful with their money. I was ashamed of where I lived in Liverpool, which is wrong. I became a bit of a snob. But I have had that knocked out of me since I came to live in Kirkby! I wouldn't let anyone denigrate the city or people of Liverpool. People here are wonderful, and they have a great community spirit.

Marie K., like Ann, loved living in Much Wenlock:

> I had a very happy time but the effects of the evacuation in the long term gave me an inferiority complex. I felt I had missed out in my education. I resented this because all my brothers had a better education than I did. Yet I had more freedom in Much Wenlock than I'd have had at home. When I returned to Liverpool I had a lot of responsibility to shoulder. My mother had got herself a little job and I was expected to help with the other children. During the war, people had to do what they thought was best for their children.

Frank, reflecting upon his time at Hednesford:

> I feel it had a number of effects on me. The fact of having lived away from home for a fairly long time — more than a year, at an impressionable age, gave me confidence in moving away from home later. For example facing up to national service.
>
> I think I returned to Liverpool with a streak of snobbishness. The evacuation had provided an alternative environment to the small back-to-back houses, living too close to factories and the docks — all creating a variety of smells that pervaded the atmosphere every day. The sub-culture of the area seemed so limiting: church , pub, cinema and work — a vicious circle that engulfed every one from an early age.
>
> I have never been a dogmatic Catholic, and I have never felt any hostility towards any other religion. I sometimes wonder if this tolerant attitude to religious belief started when I had to live in a house which included four people of four different religious persuasions.
>
> Because the evacuation was a product of the war, and because as children we had actual experience of bombing and destruction, I think it contributed to my detestation of all aspects of war. I refuse to believe that war brings glory to any country, or to any groups of people. I feel resentment when I look at war memorials and I consider them to be statements about the futility and obscenity of war.

What of those who had been on the 'receiving end' of the evacuation scheme? What impact did their involvement make upon them?

Lil, from Much Wenlock:

> The evacuation made a great impact on my family. We enjoyed the war years, not as such, but because we had the evacuees. It

opened our eyes to a lot of things. We got on exceptionally well with the children and their families. It was sad that children had to be wrenched from their families. I don't think that the Wenlock children would have been as adaptable as the Liverpool children, if the evacuation had been reversed. That's because Wenlock families are closely knit together. On the other hand the war destroyed the best years of our lives. I was in my late 'teens, and my social life was nil. I feel that the bombing of Liverpool, London and Coventry was such a waste. Those cities remained in such a mess for a long time after the war.

Rosemary, also from Much Wenlock:

The evacuation and the war made me more tolerant towards others. I was an only child, and at first I was quite jealous of our evacuee, Pauline. She seemed to get away with everything, and went short of nothing. War was very destructive. I lost three dear friends during the first twelve months — an experience like this knocks you for six! It was an utter waste. It got this country no where!

Chapter Six

REFLECTIONS AND CONCLUSIONS

In compiling this record of the war-time evacuation scheme I have been very conscious of its limitations. What I have tried to do is to reconstruct some of the arguments for introducing the national scheme in 1939, and then to allow the evacuees themselves to 'speak' about their experiences. The official documentation of the war-time period suggests that the scheme was an administrative success. An extraordinary number of civilian people were moved about the country in a short period of time. Although social research shows that the scheme encountered many problems and showed defects, the fact that so many people returned home so quickly in 1939 and 1940, was due to the quietism engendered by the 'Phoney War', rather than to any administrative failure.

But then followed the effects of the bombing of our major cities from mid-1940. The appeal to move women and children away while this was going on, met a ready response in Liverpool. These gradual phases of evacuation had important social consequences. For the first time in modern history, and on such a scale for such an extended period, city people found themselves in rural and semi-rural areas. On the other hand, small rural towns and villages found themselves virtually over-run with children from the cities. This mixing of contrasting cultures has clearly made some lasting impressions on the consciousness of the group of people I have been able to interview. The evacuation experience seemed to enlarge the world of the evacuees. Perhaps the greatest impact was felt initially at the level of family life. Children frequently belonged to two or more 'families', over an extensive period of time. Parents were willing to relinquish the care of their children to others who were complete strangers. When evacuees returned to their city they were better able to assess their own environment from a much broader context, because they had sampled life elsewhere.

Some of the interviews suggest a simplistic dichotomy between life in the city and life in rural areas: the city is dirty, the children delinquent; the countryside with its more wholesome traditions seemed to offer security and promise. The physical environment may have differed between the two, but the social conditions were often quite similar. It is significant that the majority of children returned to Liverpool and were glad to do so, but they became more critically aware of the need for social change.

The evacuation was one of the most important national experiences, along with war-time conscription, that forced politicians and social reformers to think hard about the post-war social reconstruction of Britain. The historian Jackson wrote:

> Neville Chamberlain said that he and his colleagues in the government had had no inkling that conditions in the urban working-class sections were so desperate. The evacuation pointed out these weaknesses and provided the incentive for post-war reforms in areas such as national health, housing, and adequate supplies of nutritional foods.[21]

In addition, R.A. Butler, the Minister of Edcuation in the wartime coalition government, remarked on several occasions that the social experience of the evacuation was a great spur to him in considering the reorganisation of the educational system in the 1944 Education Act.

Wartime evacuation was a unique experience not only for those who took part, but also historically. Never before in this country had so many civilians, mainly children of school age, been mobilised to move from their homes into areas designated as 'safe' from aerial attack. Some figures giving an indication of this movement, (regarded as the 'largest migration in British history'), were given in the journals of the period. Calder in his *The People's War*, calculated that 'population movements in September (1939) alone affected a quarter to a third of the population'. This was a remarkable feat.

The people I have interviewed all proved to be articulate, open-minded, and well integrated into life in the late 1980s. To what extent, if at all, have they become like this as a consequence of living away from home and family, during their early formative years? This is the tantalizing question that must terminate this discussion.

References

1.   HMSO (1938), p.5.

2.   Beasley (1949), p.55.

3.   Second Chance to Learn (1984), p.3.

4.   Mass Observation, September 3rd, 1939.

5.   Calder (1971), p.23.

6.   University of Liverpool (1939), pp. 3-5.

7.   Padley & Cole (eds) (1940), p.42.

8.   Calder, *op.cit.*, p.38.

9.   Second Chance to Learn, *op.cit.*, p.6.

10. I*bid.*

11. Calder, *op. cit.*, p.48.

12. Titmus (1950), p.179n.

13. Mass Observation, September 16th, 1939.

14. Second Chance to Learn, *op.cit.*, p.6.

15. Liverpool Daily Post & Echo/Scouse Press (1983), p.16.

16. Calder, *op.cit.*, p.246.

17. Longmate (1973), p.53.

18. Pooley (1972), pp.8-9.

19. Padley & Cole, *op.cit.*, pp.236-7.

20. Jackson (1985), p.49.

21. Jackson, *op.cit.*, pp. 22-3.

Liver Press Publications

Pat Ayers   **Women at War: Live**   **omen 1939-45**

When war was declared in ' eptemb⌐ J39, the people of Britain entered a period which ⌐ ... to ¹₋ay , lives untouched. This book tells the story of the impact of war on Liverpool women. Pay Ayers uses the memories of the women themselves to vividly recreate their experiences during that time. The laughter and tears, the drama and the everyday routine of life in wartime Liverpool are uncovered revealing the humour, strength and resources of local women.

Anthony Miller **Poverty Deserved? Relieving the Poor in Victorian Liverpool**

Behind the splendour of Victorian architecture lay the squalour of the city slums whose inhabitants suffered some of the most shocking conditions of poverty in nineteenth century Britain. This book captures the substance of the lives of the poor community in Liverpool in the face of such hardship. It examines the methods and attitudes of the city's charitable institutions in their attempt to alleviate poverty by charitable effort.

Bibliography

(i) **Primary sources**

(a) **Reports**

Preliminary Report on Problems of Evacuation, University of Liverpool Press/Hodder & Stoughton, London, 1939.

Report of Committee on Evacuation, Cmd. 5837, HMSO, 1938.

Report on Conditions in Reception Areas, HMSO, 1941.

Borough of Much Wenlock Minute Book 1928-1944.

Much Wenlock Sanitary Committee Book 1938-1941.

(b) **Surveys and other publications**

Beasley, H.C., *The Fortieth Jewel, St. Gerard's 1915-1949*, published by Rev. D.J. Kelly, PP., Liverpool 1949.

Liverpool Daily Post & Echo/Scouse Press, *Bombers Over Merseyside*, Liverpool 1983.

Mass Observation : Extract From Diary, September 1939.

Padley, R., & Cole, M. (eds), *Evacuation Survey*, Routledge & Sons, London, 1940.

Titmus, R., *Problems of Social Policy* HMSO, 1950.

(ii) **Secondary sources**

Calder, Angus, *The People's War : Britain 1939-1945*, Granada Publications, London (1971 edition).

Jackson, Carlton, *Who Will Take Our Children?*, Methuen, London, 1985.

Longmate, Norman, *How We Lived Then*, Arrow Books, London, 1971.

Pooley, R., *The Evacuees*, Anglo-American Press, Hull, 1972.

Second Chance to Learn, *Merseyside Women's War*, Liverpool, 1984.

Waugh, Evelyn, *Put Out More Flags*, Penguin Books, London, 1942.